WHERE ARE ALL THE BROTHERS?

WHERE ARE ALL THE BROTHERS?

STRAIGHT ANSWERS TO MEN'S QUESTIONS ABOUT THE CHURCH

ERIC C. REDMOND

CROSSWAY BOOKS

WHEATON, ILLINOIS

Mobipocket ISBN: 978-1-4335-0459-4

PDF ISBN: 978-1-4335-0458-7

Library of Congress Cataloging-in-Publication Data
Redmond, Eric C.
  Where are all the brothers? / straight answers to men's questions about the church / Eric C. Redmond
     p. cm.
  Includes bibliographical references.
  ISBN 978-1-4335-0178-4 (tpb)
    1. African American men—Religious life. 2. African Americans—
Religion. I. Title.
BR563.N4R43   2008
277.3'083081—dc22   2007044602

CH		17	16	15	14	13	12	11	10	09	08
14	13	12	11	10	9	8	7	6	5	4	3	2	1

To Pamela,
my Autumn

CONTENTS

ACKNOWLEDGMENTS

The Lord has been most gracious and kind to me through his Son, Jesus Christ, my Savior. I stand in awe and humility before him daily as I think of his goodness toward me through many people who have helped bring this project to fruition.

Special thanks to Laureece Hymes, Ted Griffin, and Mark Scott, who aided me with some very fine editing. Thank you to Castello Bentley, Sam Hodges, Quincy Jones, Muriel Matthis-Lyles, Alfreda McAdams, Shirley Russell, and Rev. Greg Sims, who all read the earliest draft of the manuscript.

Thabiti Anyabwile, Anthony Carter, Ronald Crawford, Cameron Shoulders, Stacy Scott, James Wilson, and Curtis Woods each read a later edition of the work. Their red ink and pencil marks helped make this work much better than the original.

I am grateful for the members of Hillcrest Baptist Church who give me grace as their shepherd. Also, I am a debtor to a host of people at First Baptist Church of Highland Park who reared me in the ministry as schoolmasters, giving me a foundation for all of my service and loving me through the years I was cutting my teeth at their expense.

To my small group, my prayer group, and many others who prayed: I could not have done this without you holding me up before the Lord. I hope you will enjoy the fruit of grace upon your prayers.

My graduate and undergraduate Black Church Ministry professors Eddie B. Lane and Bernard Fuller added fodder to a burning passion for revitalization in the African-American church. Special thanks goes to Professor Lane who said, "The poorest of people need the best of theologians." I must also give thanks to the Lord for the roles of Mark Dever, Larry Mercer, and Paige Patterson in this work. Al Fisher and Jill Carter, too, have been kind friends to me since the idea for this project first arrived at Crossway.

I have the greatest parents in the world, Walter and Linda Redmond. This small space is not enough to thank them for the ways in which they continue to pour their love into my life. It has been my hope to be able to put my thanks to you in print for the entire world to see. You, the real "Dr. Redmond" and the lady who pretended to lance my foot in order to help me memorize U.S. state capitals in the second grade, are my heroes. I love you both.

I also have the greatest set of children in the world. The Five C's bring me great joy daily. Thank you for praying for Daddy's book project and rejoicing with him at its completion. It is definitely time to make a week's worth of runs to the ice cream shop.

Finally, this project would not have been possible at all without the wife of every man's dreams sharing the hope and supporting the work from conception to completion. Pam, you have made this journey so much fun for me, as you have done for everything in my life for the last nineteen years. I wish every married couple could share the love, joy, and belonging to one another that we share. I dedicate this book to you, my Autumn, with whom I am several steps beyond friendship.

INTRODUCTION

What You Will Gain If You Give Me Ten Minutes of Your Life for Each of the Next Nine Days

Giving me ten minutes of your life for each of the next nine days could change your whole life. It could make life better than it ever has been. It could also make an eternal difference.

"Yeah, yeah, brother . . . I've heard it all before," you protest. But if I may say so, the words above are not empty promises but words of hope, for your sake. For if you have this booklet in your hands, it means that someone is concerned for your well-being. That someone intends for you to see life from another perspective. Someone is concerned for your heart, mind, and soul.

Either you do not go to church, or you attend infrequently, or you go to a church that the person who gave you this booklet perhaps judges to be harmful rather than beneficial to you. You have your reasons for your type of church attendance—all reasons that are legitimate to you. These might include your experiences with church as a child or an adult, your study of religion, your contact with so-called "Christians" who consistently attend church but whose lives do not seem to match their declarations of faith. Or maybe you have had contact with people of other faiths whose lives appear to conform better to their confessions. Based on these experiences, you dismiss church as a sham or settle for giving up two hours on Sunday so your children will have some religion and your wife will leave you alone!

If you have been thinking any of these thoughts, you are not alone. I would like to talk with you about your reasons for not giving church (or a different church) another chance. I believe that you are right in your observations. But I request ten minutes so that we may follow the path of your conclusions to stops further down the road.

If you will accept the challenge to read this book with me, what you will find is truth that can lead you to have success and satisfaction in your own life:

• You say church is for women and not for men. I will show you why church is for men just like you.

• You are turned off by the preacher who fattens his purse through the giving of others. But I will show you how to find a real church with a preacher whose life matches up to the biblical standard for a man of God.

• You think the church is weak compared to followers of Islam. I will show you how your view of Islam should make you take another hard look at the potential might of the church—a potential that you hold in your hands.

• You have found organized religion a hindrance to your faith in any God. I will explain to you how organized religion has benefits that you have overlooked that could radically improve your life.

• You say that you do not know about the Jesus people preach. I will talk to you about who and what Jesus himself claimed to be and do.

My hope in offering you this book is that a transformation will take place in your life. My hope and prayer for all who read this book is a reformation—that an army of African-American men will make their way back into the church, back into the leadership of the church, back into leading a change in the church to be and do what it is called to be and do, so that we may have power to do good for our people, and people all over the world, in a way that no government or service organization has been or will be able to do, and that no one will be able to take away.

I think you will enjoy the trip through these pages. To make the readings most enjoyable, may I suggest a manner for gaining the most from this book:

1. Set aside a ten-minute time period to read each day and for reflecting on the reading.

2. Beginning with the first day's reading, read one chapter a day for nine days in a row, starting today. If you put the book down for a period of time and do not get to it daily, that's okay. Simply pick up where you left off when you begin reading again.

3. Think about your answers to the "Things to Consider" questions immediately after reading the chapter.

4. Over the course of the nine days, you may wish to consider a church to visit, keeping in mind what you have read and pondered.

5. When you have finished the book, give a second look at the chapters you deem of greatest importance, then pick two or three

issues about which to think further. I have provided a "For Further Study" section at the end of each reading in order to point you to resources to help you in your search for the truth.

My prayer for you on this nine-day journey is that you will see that you have every reason to go to church, that you will go to a good church, that you will greatly enjoy being there, and that your presence there will result in the redemption of many in your community and around the world.

The rest is on you.

If you are willing to accept the challenge, let us begin reading.

"Not everyone who says to me, 'Lord, Lord,'
will enter the kingdom of heaven,
but the one who does the will of my Father
who is in heaven."

MATTHEW 7:21

"Or those eighteen on whom the tower in Siloam fell
and killed them: do you think that they were
worse offenders than all the others who lived in
Jerusalem? No, I tell you; but unless you repent,
you will all likewise perish."

LUKE 13:4–5

ISN'T THE CHURCH FULL OF HYPOCRITES?

The church is full of a bunch of hypocrites who are simply looking for a crutch to make it through life. I have seen such people, just as you have:

• They sing, shout, and wave their hands on Sunday but curse you out later that week.

• They exalt humility as a virtue but wear the finest clothes and drive the nicest cars as status symbols, and they look down on those who cannot.

• They are deacons, stewards, trustees, elders, and preachers who are supposed to set the example for the people but can be regularly seen leaving the corner store with a brown bag that is not concealing pork rinds.

• They say they love Jesus but abuse their children, cannot mend a relationship with an estranged family member, or are the worst workers in the office.

• They repeatedly tell you and everyone else that you need to be "saved" or "born again" and are judgmental of your every word or lifestyle, never seeing that their attitudes need to be "saved."

These apparent contradictions in thought and action suggest to you that nothing has truly happened inside those churchgoers' hearts. You do not see the spiritual transformation they claim to have. You even may have thought to yourself that if those people represent what it means to be a Christian or a church member, then you do not need to live such a lie. You would be right!

In fact, your observations make some marvelous and significant assumptions:

1. A claim of a belief should follow through with practice of that belief. That is, a person's belief should influence his behavior.

2. Churches should be full of those whose claims and practices match, and churches should be without those whose claims and practices do not match—those who are hypocrites.

I would agree with you, and I would understand your skepticism where these two standards are absent.

However, this would also mean that you yourself must have a claim of belief that matches your practice of that belief (or you would be guilty of the very thing of which you accuse them). You yourself are without exception one of the following types of persons:

1. *Righteous*—one who believes he is a good and righteous person and therefore practices right and good all the time (or at least tries to). This is the only type of person who is both good and without hypocrisy in belief and actions.

2. *Wicked*—one who believes he is an evil and uncaring person who practices evil and unkindness. This is the only type of person who is both evil and without hypocrisy in belief and actions.

3. *Hypocritical*—one who believes he is a good and righteous person but practices evil and unkindness. This is the self-righteous

hypocrite who has caused you to be skeptical of church people. But church people are not the only ones who suffer from this flaw. Most people are hypocrites in this way, for most people tend to think of themselves as good people who do not harm others. All people, however, are guilty of evil or unkindness, even if it is to the smallest degree known to man, even if it is only an evil or unkind thought. People who are truly good and righteous cannot have even one evil thought.

4. *Weak*—one who believes he is an evil and uncaring person but believes he practices righteousness and good at all times. In theory, this person can exist. But he would have serious mental, emotional, and spiritual problems.

Truthfully, the Bible teaches that we are all wicked in the sight of God, for "none is righteous, no, not one" (Rom. 3:10). God's standard of righteousness is higher than ours. Before him, we each are practical hypocrites, thinking we are righteous in his sight but actually practicing deeds of wickedness.

In person-to-person dealings, you may be an individual who believes he is a good and righteous person and therefore practices right and good all the time (or at least tries to). Or at least I hope you are! If so, you would be the ideal church member. You would be the ideal follower of God, one who could help others. Many like you who are not hypocrites would set an example for other people to follow. Together we could be the model of churchgoers who both claim and know the holy and righteous God, who have turned away from living sinfully and have turned to living according to God's standards of practice as revealed in his Word, the Bible.

If this is so, why don't you find a local church of which you can be a member, learn more of God's Word, and live according to his standards of practice? The church would be glad to have you.

THINGS TO CONSIDER

1. Read the verses cited at the beginning of this chapter (Matthew 7:21; Luke 13:4–5). What does Matthew 7:21 tell you about God's view of hypocrites?
2. What does Luke 13:4–5 tell us about the danger of seeing sin in others but not in oneself? How can these verses help you to examine yourself before criticizing others?
3. What might you gain if you went to church and studied God's Word to the point that you could correct a hypocrite and people would begin to see a truly righteous way to live?

FOR FURTHER STUDY

Ellis, Carl. *Free at Last? The Gospel in the African-American Experience.* Downers Grove, IL: InterVarsity Press, 1995.

*No prophecy of Scripture comes from someone's own
interpretation. For no prophecy was ever produced
by the will of man, but men spoke from God as
they were carried along by the Holy Spirit.*

2 PETER 1:20–21

*Our beloved brother Paul also wrote to you according
to the wisdom given him, as he does in all his letters
when he speaks in them of these matters. There are
some things in them that are hard to understand,
which the ignorant and unstable twist to their own
destruction, as they do the other Scriptures.*

2 PETER 3:15–16

*And we also thank God constantly for this,
that when you received the word of God,
which you heard from us, you accepted it not as
the word of men but as what it really is,
the word of God, which is at work in you believers.*

1 THESSALONIANS 2:13

WASN'T THE BIBLE WRITTEN BY MEN?

The Bible is a book written by men. We even know many of them by their names.

Moses was one of the writers of Scripture: "If you believed Moses, you would believe me; for he wrote of me," said Jesus in John 5:46. We also read, "And beginning with Moses and all the Prophets, he interpreted to them in all the Scriptures the things concerning himself" (Luke 24:27). That is, Jesus explained to his listeners that the writings of Moses, which are the books Genesis through Deuteronomy in the Bible, could be used as a compass to guide them to him.

Joshua, Moses' lieutenant, was one of the contributors to Scripture. "And Joshua wrote these words in the Book of the Law of God," we are told in Joshua 24:26–27.

David, the second king of Israel, was a tremendous writer of a portion of the Scriptures. More than twenty-five chapters of the Psalms begin with "A Psalm of David" (see, for example, Psalms 51 and 68).

Solomon, David's son and also a great king of Israel, contributed most of the proverbs found in the book of Proverbs: "The proverbs of Solomon, son of David, king of Israel" (Prov. 1:1).

Paul the apostle wrote at least thirteen of the New Testament books. The apostle Peter says of him, "And count the patience of our Lord as salvation, just as our beloved brother Paul also wrote to you according to the wisdom given him, as he does in all his letters when he speaks in them of these matters. There are some things in them that are hard to understand, which the ignorant and unstable twist to their own destruction, as they do the other Scriptures" (2 Pet. 3:15–16).

The stories of these men are commonly known, many even being made into movies (e.g., *The Ten Commandments* and *David and Bathsheba*). They were real men—fathers, brothers, sons, farmers, warriors, teachers, fishermen, and kings. They were much like you and me.

In fact, they were just like you and me, as their recorded failures show us:

- Moses killed a man and purposely disobeyed God.
- Joshua was deceived because of a failure to pray for guidance.
- David was an adulterer, murderer, and calculating deceiver.
- Solomon was full of himself, building his residential house to be larger than God's house.
- Jeremiah decided that he would not preach for God anymore.
- John had a problem with vengeance.
- James, the brother of Jesus, rejected Jesus' claim to be Messiah until after Jesus' death.
- Paul was a violent man who blasphemed God and had Christians killed because they were Christians, which to Paul—prior to his conversion to Christianity—was a threat to the purity of Judaism.

If the Bible were left in the hands of these men alone—murderers, adulterers, deceivers, doubters, blasphemers, rebels, and violent men (a list of men who sound like they should be put away for sixty to life)—you would have every ground to be suspicious of their ability to write or say anything about God!

If the task of writing Scripture were left to their hands alone, your concern is a valid one. Men like this would not be the most trusted bunch to deliver perfect truth.

Your concern for truth is commendable. I say this because you presume the following:

1. The Bible should be a document of absolute truth if it is to fulfill the claim that it is God's holy Word.

2. Men would remain capable of misinformation, corruption, error, or even spin—everything except absolute truth—if left alone as writers.

3. If the Bible is a work of truth, then it is the most important truth there is, one worthy for you to read.

But please also consider the following:

1. Although men wrote the Bible, the Bible claims to be a document of truth containing accurately recorded history by many eyewitnesses—eyewitnesses who gave testimony of the events—not misinformation:

> This is the disciple who is bearing witness about these things, and who has written these things. (John 21:24)

> [Christ] was raised on the third day . . . [Christ] appeared to Cephas, then to the twelve. Then he appeared to more than five hundred brothers at one time, most of whom are still alive, though some have fallen asleep. Then he appeared to James,

then to all the apostles. Last of all, as to one untimely born, he
appeared also to me. (1 Cor. 15:4–8)

We did not follow cleverly devised myths when we made known
to you the power and coming of our Lord Jesus Christ, but we
were eyewitnesses of his majesty. (2 Pet. 1:16)

2. Although men wrote the Bible across several centuries—
Moses in the 1500s B.C.; David around 1000 B.C.; Solomon in the
900s B.C.; Jeremiah in the 600s and 500s B.C.; Paul, James, and John
in the first century A.D.—all wrote accurately about the same thing
as the one unifying idea of Scripture: the Person of Jesus Christ and
his work to redeem mankind from sin to God. In doing so, many
foretold of his birth, earthly ministry, death, and resurrection with
100 percent accuracy. The chances of the prophecies being fulfilled
in this manner are $1/1x10^{100}$ (1 to 1 followed by 100 zeros)!

3. Although the Bible was written by men, they wrote of their
own flaws and the consequences of those flaws. This would suggest
that the writers were credible, for they did not try to hide informa-
tion or polish themselves to make their lives appear to be perfect. In
contrast, if we had been the authors, we might have edited our own
failures right out of the story! Or at least we might have written
that God says life is one big party, so live it up! Or we might have
written that we always pleased God and never sinned against him.
Mere human writers would definitely have removed fornication,
adultery, gluttony, stealing, lying, gossiping, and greed from their
list of sins! Most certainly, mere human writers would not have
made us responsible for the crucifixion of the Son of God!

4. Although the Bible was written by men, the Bible also lays claim to have been written by God, for the Bible says, "all Scripture is breathed out by God" (2 Tim. 3:16), and "no prophecy was ever produced by the will of man, but men spoke from God as they were carried along by the Holy Spirit" (2 Pet. 1:21). Ultimately and intimately, it is God who used men as the human writers of his spoken word. And God safeguarded the writing of his spoken word so that it was free from human error. (See the recommended reading at the end of this chapter.)

5. Although the Bible has its origin in God, he did not override the will of men so completely that the gifts, personalities, and experiences of each do not show through their writings. Instead, the individuality of each of these men is expressed through his writing, allowing for the readers of the Bible to identify with different sections of Scripture during different life stages, to enjoy the beauty of the creativity of God, and to marvel at the grace of God! Just think of what it means for you or me that God chose to use farmers and shepherds and so on—not just teachers, but also men with no formal scholastic training, not just the faithful, but also the faltering! The fact that God worked with men to give his Word to us is not a slight against the Word of God but is an example of the great kindness of God to trust us with his Word.

Therefore, my brother, the truth—God's Word—is available and is not distorted by the hands of men. So find a copy of the Bible so you can read the written words of God. Therein you will find the message of life. The same God who worked through men to give you his very words became a man to address your need to know him through repentance from sin and faith in the Son of God and his work to pay for your sins and rose again to offer you eternal life. This is God's final word "written" for man.

THINGS TO CONSIDER

1. If the Bible is God's very own words, what may be the benefit of reading and understanding God's Word?
2. Sometimes the Bible seems difficult to understand because we use translations or versions of the Bible written in the standard language of a time centuries before us (e.g., the King James Version). Or it may be that we are using a Bible written at a reading level above our own. Try reading a Bible that uses simpler language, such as the English Standard Version (ESV), the version used in this writing, available from Crossway Bibles (www.esv.org).
3. The next time you pick up your Bible to read it, try starting with Mark (see the Table of Contents in your Bible). It is a short, easy-to-read account about the life of Jesus and his ministry in service to mankind.
4. Read some each day until you are finished. You may find God's Word speaking to you.

FOR FURTHER STUDY

Bruce, F. F. *The New Testament Documents: Are They Reliable?* Grand Rapids, MI: Eerdmans, 2003.

Fee, Gordon and Douglas Stuart. *How to Read the Bible for All Its Worth.* Grand Rapids, MI: Zondervan, 2003.

Kaiser, Walter C. *The Old Testament Documents: Are They Reliable? Are They Relevant?* Downers Grove, IL: InterVarsity Press, 2002.

*I desire then that in every place the men should pray,
lifting holy hands without anger or quarreling.*
1 TIMOTHY 2:8

*Do not rebuke an older man but encourage him
as you would a father.*
1 TIMOTHY 5:1

*And what you have heard from me in the
presence of many witnesses entrust to faithful men
who will be able to teach others also.*
2 TIMOTHY 2:2

ISN'T THE CHURCH GEARED TOWARD WOMEN?

The church does seem to be geared toward women. One does not need to look far to see this:

• The expressive show of emotion—the shouting, clapping, and swaying—is common to and more comfortable for women. Such expressiveness seems to fit the way women are made.

• The emphasis on meekness, gentleness, and patience in the lives of men seems to encourage women to walk all over men on account of men's perceived passivity.

• The beat-up-on-men sermons that emphasize what black men are not, don't have, and don't do appear to reinforce a concept that men are weak (even in God's sight) and that women are the strong ones who do all of the work in home and church.

If that weren't bad enough, one might also consider:

• The apparent demeaning of sexual prowess in sermons on sexual immorality.

• The lack of challenge from the pulpit to women to hold their tongues, be busy at home, submit to their husbands, and show respect to their husbands.

• The lack of sports and labor activities for men in the church.

All in all, the whole concept of church—Sunday worship, weekly activities, and membership—seems like one big women's society, with (in most cases) a man at the helm with a message to get women to follow what he says. But often the women are not equipped and empowered to talk respectfully, quietly, meekly, to support decisions concerning discipline of the children, to understand how men cope with the stress of very hard jobs differently than women do, or to give words of honor for hard work or faithfulness by a good man, husband, or father—a man, husband, or father that most women would love!

Add the fact that male homosexual behavior is ignored for the sake of a good music program and church seems like no more than a glorified hair salon or day spa. Women come, get pampered, receive a feminine pep talk, are allowed to express themselves, laugh as brothers are verbally emasculated, smile as Harry with a purse says, "Go, girl," pay their money, and leave until their appointment next week!

While I have humorously exaggerated what the typical church scene is like, I am trying to let you know that you have put your finger on something true, real, and skewed. Your feeling about women-centered church is really asking, "Shouldn't church, if it is truly the house of God for all people, a) seek to effect life transformation for both men and women, b) speak to the issues of concern to both men and women, c) make home better for men as well as for women, and d) have gatherings that are exciting and comfortable to both men and women?"

The answer to your question is, "Yes!" Indeed, God has laid out in the Bible a plan that places a priority on building up men to become strong leaders in the home and in the church:

• Men are called to be the heads of households, and their wives are to respect them: "Wives, submit to your own husbands, as to the Lord. For the husband is the head of the wife even as Christ is the head of the church, his body, and is himself its Savior. Now as the church submits to Christ, so also wives should submit in everything to their husbands" (Eph. 5:22–24).

• Men are to be pastors, elders, and deacons—the primary leaders in the church (1 Tim. 3:1–7; Titus 1:5–9): "This is why I left you in Crete, so that you might put what remained into order, and appoint elders in every town as I directed you—if anyone is above reproach, the husband of one wife, and his children are believers and not open to the charge of debauchery or insubordination" (Titus 1:5–6). Such leaders should be sensitive to issues affecting both men and women. However, the people are to follow men.

• Men were the leaders in ancient Israel as tribal heads, prophets, priests, kings, sages, choirmasters, songwriters, warriors, and gatekeepers. There are some exceptions to this in Scripture, such as Deborah the judge (leader). But such examples are only exceptions; overwhelmingly, men hold all leadership positions among God's people. In the case of Deborah, she only came to rule because Barak failed to lead as God called him to do and was judged accordingly (Judg. 4).

• The disciples taught by Jesus to lead the church were men (Matt. 10:1–2). Later becoming the thirteen apostles—after the death of Judas and the addition of Matthias and Paul—these men stood in authority over the elders in matters of establishing new churches, appointing church leadership, shepherding God's people, and settling matters of dispute in the church (Acts 8:14–17; 15:2, 22; 21:17–25).

• Men are to search for faithful men who will teach the Word of God in order to pass down the faith to the next generation (2 Tim. 2:1–2).

• Men are to be examples to all people in the congregation (Titus 2:1–2, 6–8).

• Men are to train their children, and the children are to obey them (Eph. 6:1–4).

God intends for men to lead and to love, so that members of the family and the church may find comfort, identity, purpose, and connectedness.

So if it is a church made for men and women for which you are looking, but you cannot seem to find one, it is not because God designed the church to be women-led or women-centered. It is because you, and many brothers like you, are needed to fill places at church and take their God-given, Scripture-prescribed roles as leaders—as pastors, elders, preachers, teachers, deacons, older men who are respected, wisdom-giving example-setters, disciple-makers, loving husbands, and nurturing fathers. So go take your place, with your concern for the church to become an exciting and comfortable place for men—real men. We need you now more than ever.

THINGS TO CONSIDER

1. Consider the three Scripture verses at the beginning of today's reading. How do each of their teachings compare to what you have seen in church in your experience?

2. What might be the benefit to the African-American society at large if a great number of men were to learn God's role and place for men and live it out in the home, the workplace, the church, and every neighborhood? (Consider some of the problems faced by today's young people or the economically disadvantaged.)

FOR FURTHER STUDY

Lane, Eddie B. *Reclaiming the Village: The African American Christian Man*. Dallas: Black Family Press, 1998.

Piper, John. *What's the Difference? Manhood and Womanhood Defined According to the Bible*. Wheaton, IL: Crossway Books, 2001.

*The saying is trustworthy: If anyone aspires to
the office of overseer, he desires a noble task.
Therefore an overseer must be above reproach,
the husband of one wife. . . . He must manage his own
household well, with all dignity keeping his children
submissive, for if someone does not know how to
manage his own household, how will he
care for God's church?*

1 TIMOTHY 3:1–2, 4–5

*Do not admit a charge against an elder except on the
evidence of two or three witnesses. As for those who
persist in sin, rebuke them in the presence of all,
so that the rest may stand in fear.*

1 TIMOTHY 5:19–20

*For an overseer, as God's steward, must be above
reproach . . . self-controlled, upright, holy,
and disciplined.*

TITUS 1:7–8

ISN'T THE PREACHER JUST A MAN?

The man you see preaching from the pulpit is just a man! When he was nine years old, he played on the boys' club seventy-five-pound football team with you. He skipped school a few days in tenth grade just like you and your friends. He has had to apply for work in the past—busing tables, serving burgers, selling newspapers, and loading parcel trucks. He disobeyed his mom and dad when he was a child. He has yelled at his children, has eaten too much sweet potato pie at Thanksgiving, and has overworked when his wife wanted him home.

The man you have seen preaching has to brush his teeth, clean bathrooms, bust suds, call a plumber, mow his own lawn, visit his doctor, and put down the remote control once in a while. He has to get sleep and pay bills. He probably loves his car, and he eats his share of fried fish, fried potatoes, fried chicken, chitterlings, and (in some cases) hog mogs too! Truthfully, he is just another brother trying to make it through this journey. Simply because at some point in his life he began to get serious about church and God and then started preaching, you think you have no reason to believe that guy is not the same ol' Snoop, Peanut, Junior, Scooter, Pee-Wee or J.J. you knew from the neighborhood.

I must admit, it would be hard for me to follow another mortal like myself, knowing my common human faults. It would also be hard for me to give a man (and his preached word) more respect than my own words when he is made out of the same stuff as any other man. But what prompts me to give a preacher another serious look is this: he, supposedly, is not made only out of the stuff that is in any other man. The man you look at weekly in the pulpit should be distinguished from other men by the composite of these six characteristics:

1. *Conversion.* The preacher should be one who has turned away from a life of sin, has professed faith in Christ, and has demonstrated a lifestyle consistent with the moral standards of Scripture. He should have an experience that changes him from a rebel against God to a follower of God. He should be like Moses, who in his burning bush experience with God was transformed from a fugitive fearful of leading God's people into a shepherd described as "very meek, more than all people who were on the face of the earth" (Num. 12:3). He should be like Paul, who after his Damascus Road encounter with Christ went from being a persecutor of the church to one who "preach[ed] the faith he once tried to destroy" (Gal. 1:23). The preacher should no longer just be Snoop but a man who has met God and fears him.

2. *Vocation.* A man who proclaims the Word of God should be called by God. This does not mean that he heard an audible voice from heaven, saw "go preach" in the clouds, had a dream that he should preach, or even that because his brothers, daddy, and granddaddy were preachers he should be one automatically. But the preacher should have a settled conviction that God has told his heart and mind that he has a special work for him to do in ministry. He should have an experience like Moses, who was

marked out for God's service at birth, or like Jeremiah, who was marked out for God's service prior to birth (see Exod. 2:1–10; Jer. 1:1–10). Or he should have an experience like Peter, who was directly commissioned by Christ to "feed my sheep," or like Paul, whose calling was spoken by God to a man named Ananias and was then given to Paul (John 21:15–17; Acts 9:15–17). Just as we often observe the superb skills of some athletes, entertainers, and musicians and say, "He was born to throw down the rock," "he was made for the sax," or "he ain't been nothing but a dancer from birth," we should observe that God has marked out and fitted certain men for pastoral leadership. As is often traditional in African-American churches, this means that the man will become a preacher. This may seem subjective, for any man could claim to have had a call from God. However, items 3–6 act as checks and balances to protect people from the phonies and charlatans.

3. *Education.* Because the preacher is a man who helps lead people in following God by teaching them the Word of God, the preacher must be one who has sound understanding of the Holy Scriptures, an understanding that greatly exceeds the knowledge of his students. The preacher must be one who can be thorough and certain in what he teaches and preaches. While the Bible does not require such depth to come from a formal source like a Bible college or seminary, many churches do. Men are needed to teach people the deep truths about God so that God might be esteemed far above the destructive, simple pleasures and sins that this life readily offers. Generally it is formally trained men who have this

ability. I say generally because you may know of exceptions—men with no formal training who have tremendous knowledge of the Word of God, theology, biblical languages, and church history. But these are exceptions. The preacher should seek to gain as much understanding of God's Word, theology, biblical languages, history, church dynamics, preaching, and ministry as possible. Then you can be certain of his ability to lead you in truth.

4. *Reputation*. Prior to becoming one who holds a place of pastoral leadership, the preacher should meet a standard of character qualifications. These qualifications, as prescribed in the Bible, should place him, as a man of God, in a class by himself, above reproach:

> *The saying is trustworthy: If anyone aspires to the office of overseer, he desires a noble task. Therefore an overseer must be above reproach, the husband of one wife, sober-minded, self-controlled, respectable, hospitable, able to teach. (1 Tim. 3:1–2)*

> *This is why I left you in Crete, so that you might put what remained into order, and appoint elders in every town as I directed you—if anyone is above reproach, the husband of one wife, and his children are believers and not open to the charge of debauchery or insubordination. For an overseer, as God's steward, must be above reproach. He must not be arrogant or quick-tempered or a drunkard or violent or greedy for gain, but hospitable, a lover of good, self-controlled, upright, holy, and disciplined. (Titus 1:5–8)*

In every area in which his character can be tested, people

should observe that he is faithful, truthful, and without sin. Particular emphasis is placed on his fidelity toward women, including his faithfulness toward his wife. This aspect of a preacher's life is so significant to God that the Scripture prescribes more than twenty separate areas in which the church should do a background check before affirming someone to be qualified to lead God's people. Even if a man can "sho' nuff preach," "say a word," "tell a story," or "preach like nobody's business," his character is the backbone of his message and ministry. The skepticism that people feel toward preachers often occurs because some churches fail to give the most serious consideration to the reputation of the preacher prior to putting him up to preach. Churches must fully analyze the character of those claiming to be called by God. If churches are faithful to look past the gloss of a dynamic orator to the core of consistent integrity, then we all might be more apt to trust the character of the preacher as a man sent by God.

5. *Ordination.* Pastoral leadership is a professional work, like teaching, engineering, flying and navigating, nursing, accounting, counseling, and practicing law or medicine. As such, just like the other fields mentioned, it requires testing and certification. In the field of ministry, this certification approves the candidate as a representative of God. For the preacher, this assessment is ordination. Ordination is a process in which a candidate for ministry should be tested on his Bible knowledge, theological depth, giftedness for ministry, ministry experience, and wisdom in decision-making. It is also a process that should be post-character examination

and post-education (see *Education* and *Reputation* above). In this process, clergymen with established reputations, education, experience, and wisdom give an oral examination to the called preacher in all of the above areas. In your experience, this may have been a public process in which the candidate was questioned and affirmed the same day in a matter of hours. In such a setting it is almost a given that the candidate will be affirmed, for a ceremony is in process and people have come to celebrate. It is also in such settings that questions about the candidate's character are rarely asked. Churches, however, should make an ordination process the clergy's equivalent of the Bar Exam, Professional Engineer Exam, or Medical Board Certifying Exam. An ordination certificate on the wall of a preacher should be a sign of trust: the man in front of you has the education, specialization, practice, and reputation to faithfully lead God's people as a pastor and preacher, and it has been certified before God and his people by men with the credentials to make such a claim.

6. *Exposition.* The preacher, as one responsible for teaching the Scriptures, the Word of God—God's very own words—should have the ability to explain clearly the meaning of passages of Scripture when he preaches. That meaning should be derived from the meaning God intended in the passage. The preacher should be able to give a verse-by-verse explanation—known as exposition—of a passage of Scripture. By explaining the Scriptures in this manner, the listener is assured that he or she is hearing God's voice through the preacher's exposition. An easy way to test whether or not a preacher has this ability is

to see if what he preaches to you can be reconstructed by you from the words of the passage preached as you go back through the passage on your own. This may seem like an unnecessary or unfamiliar requirement for the preacher. However, his ability to explain the Scriptures from Scripture itself is the only assurance you have that God's Word is being faithfully proclaimed. Great oratorical skills can "preach" the Emancipation Proclamation in a manner that makes you feel a great emotional charge. But such preaching is not proclaiming the life-changing power of God to liberate people from slavery to sin; it is not proclaiming what God means to say to us from the Scriptures. Only expositional preaching of the Scriptures has the power to transform and strengthen one's soul, for God will be speaking.

So if Scooter has all of the above, he's not just a man—he is a man of God. He's not just making things up when he speaks—he is preaching the Word of God. He is not simply the same as anyone else—he is a steward of souls who is accountable to God.

Go find the preacher as prescribed above, even if you have to travel between twenty-five and fifty miles (or twenty to forty-five minutes) to hear him every week. Once you meet someone with the whole package of goods—conversion, vocation, education, reputation, ordination, and exposition—go listen to him preach for several Sundays in a row. Open a Bible, and follow along as he preaches. Soon you will find yourself confronted by the very words of God from one who has been affirmed as having been called by God.

THINGS TO CONSIDER

First Timothy 3:1–7 lists qualifications for pastors. Read through that list, and see if you know of any preacher in your experience who has met these qualifications. What might your life be like if you followed that preacher's teaching and living?

FOR FURTHER STUDY

Begg, Alistair. *Preaching for God's Glory*. Wheaton, IL: Crossway Books, 1999.

Piper, John. *Brothers, We Are Not Professionals: A Plea to Pastors for a Radical Ministry*. Nashville: Broadman & Holman, 2002.

Piper, John. *The Supremacy of God in Preaching*. Grand Rapids, MI: Baker, 2004.

*Now there were in the church at Antioch prophets
and teachers, Barnabas, Simeon who was called Niger,
Lucius of Cyrene, Manaen a member of the
court of Herod the tetrarch, and Saul.*
ACTS 13:1

*And as they led him away, they seized one Simon of
Cyrene, who was coming in from the country,
and laid on him the cross, to carry it behind Jesus.*
LUKE 23:26

*And they compelled a passerby, Simon of Cyrene,
who was coming in from the country, the father of
Alexander and Rufus, to carry his cross.*
MARK 15:21

Greet Rufus, chosen in the Lord.
ROMANS 16:13

DOESN'T ISLAM OFFER MORE FOR BLACK MEN?

Islam seems to offer more for the black man than Christianity. Possibly the form of Islam with which you are most familiar is the Nation of Islam or an offshoot. If so, you may have been impressed by what you have seen of Islam for one or more of the following reasons:

• You have heard the leaders of local mosques be far more vocal on political issues that matter to you and to the majority of African-Americans.

• You see drug dealers being run out of the neighborhood by the members of the local mosque, and you are appreciative.

• You are grateful for the cleanliness and productivity of young men you see in the median selling bean pies and *The Final Call* as entrepreneurs.

• You may have experienced the brotherhood of the Nation behind bars.

• Depending on your age, you even may have heard Elijah Muhammad or Malcolm X speak in person and were inspired to become a strong man by one or both of them. You might have had a similar experience by reading *The Autobiography of Malcolm X* or by watching Spike Lee's movie *Malcolm X.*

All of this is more than you can say you have seen coming from black churches and so-called Christians. Black church members and Christians claim "thus saith the Lord," profess to be "saved, sanctified, and filled with the Holy Ghost," and preach hellfire and brimstone upon the wicked. But you see large sums of money going into their church buildings and decor, little money or work affecting the local neighborhood, and lives no more victorious day-to-day than those of people who do not make a claim to know God. You also may have seen some who seem to show no fear of God, at least not the outward fear you have seen in the neatly dressed men at the local mosque. In addition, you may have been turned off by the "whiteness" of Christianity, including the common portrayal of some of the greatest figures in the Bible as people of European descent. In your mind you may have been thinking, *If everything I see in the whole Christian religion is white, how can that work for me?*

I want you to know that your experience is not isolated. Many people have similar apprehensions concerning the church and Islam. In your experience, one religion presents itself as far more "religious" than the other. In your dealings, you can identify with the leading figures of one religion far more than the other. Your choice of Islam over the church therefore assumes that if a religion offers something credible, practical, and visible, it should be pursued over something that is incredulous, impractical, and invisible. Your leaning toward the Nation (or any form of Islam) may also assume that if a religion is not for whites but for blacks, then that is the religion for you as a black man.

Let me assure you, however, that your second concern (about the "whiteness" of Christianity) arises from misguided interpreters of the Scriptures and Christian history. For since the beginning of Christianity, and throughout church history, people of African descent have been part of the forefront of Christianity and the church.

In Scripture, Simon of Cyrene (located in modern Libya) was pulled out of a crowd to help carry the cross for Jesus Christ (Matt. 27:32; Mark 15:21; Luke 23:26). Later tradition identifies his two sons as leaders in the church at Rome and friends of the apostle Paul (cf. Rom. 16:13).

Niger (whose name means "black") and Lucius, two men of African descent, were part of the leadership of prophets and teachers in Antioch who heard the Lord speak about the church's work expanding beyond Judea and Samaria (Acts 13:1–4). They were in the group that commissioned the apostle Paul and Barnabas and sent them to far regions with the gospel to convert people to Christ. Assuming they stayed in leadership in Antioch, they were also those to whom Paul and Barnabas reported about their missions work.

There were people from Libya and other African regions present on the day of Pentecost—the day the church began (Acts 2:1–11). From the beginning we have been part of Christianity and the church.

In addition, some of the most important figures in church history have come from Africa:

• Tertullian (ca. A.D. 150–230): An early defender of the Christian faith, Tertullian was the first church father to write in Latin. Tertullian, a lawyer, was a native of Carthage in North Africa.

• Origen (ca. A.D. 180–250): Head of a Christian school in

Alexandria, Egypt, for almost three decades, Origen was a prolific writer on theology, interpretation, and Bible commentaries. He was the famed author of the Hexpla, a six-column comparison of different translations of the Old Testament.

• Athanasius (A.D. 298–373): The Bishop of Alexandria was the chief defender against the heresy of Arianism at the First Council of Nicea. Arius denied the deity of Jesus Christ. Athanasius' argumentation helped to formulate the Nicean Creed and to codify orthodox doctrine on the Trinity.

• Augustine (A.D. 354–430): The Bishop of Hippo in North Africa, Augustine is best known for his *Confessions*, *The City of God*, *On Christian Doctrine*, the *Enchiridion* on faith, hope, and love, and critical thinking that contributed to the development of the "just war theory," still utilized by Western nations. Augustine's teachings on the role of grace in salvation provided the theological backbone for the Protestant Reformation.

As you can see, people of African descent have played a great role in the Christian faith from the very inception of the church. Far from being "white," the church has been a movement for people of all ethnic backgrounds and colors. This is in fulfillment of God's promise to his servant Abram (Abraham) to bless all peoples through him:

> Now the LORD said to Abram, "Go from your country and your kindred and your father's house to the land that I will show you. And I will make of you a great nation, and I will bless you and make your name great, so that you will be a bless-ing. I will bless those who bless you, and him who dishonors

you I will curse, and in you all the families of the earth shall be blessed." (Gen. 12:1–3)

As for your concern about the public acts of Islam versus the public acts of Christianity, consider the following: In terms of credibility, there are many people in the church whose lives demonstrate great reverence for God. You may remember an older lady in your family or an old "deacon" in your neighborhood, honest, churchgoing people who loved and helped needy people in the community. Maybe such a person has been part of your family. (Maybe such a person gave you this book!) Even if you have not known someone who acted "Christian," there are and have been many such people. But keep in mind that Christianity is not calling people to be perfect. It is calling people who are sinful to change their ways, having trusted Christ to change them through his defeat of sin by his death on the cross and his power for a new life by his resurrection from the dead:

> *What shall we say then? Are we to continue in sin that grace may abound? By no means! How can we who died to sin still live in it? Do you not know that all of us who have been baptized into Christ Jesus were baptized into his death? We were buried therefore with him by baptism into death, in order that, just as Christ was raised from the dead by the glory of the Father, we too might walk in newness of life. For if we have been united with him in a death like his, we shall certainly be united with him in a resurrection like his. We know that our old self was crucified with him in order that the body of sin might be brought to nothing, so that we would no longer*

*be enslaved to sin. For one who has died has been set free from
sin. Now if we have died with Christ, we believe that we will
also live with him. We know that Christ, being raised from the
dead, will never die again; death no longer has dominion over
him. For the death he died he died to sin, once for all, but the
life he lives he lives to God. So you also must consider yourselves
dead to sin and alive to God in Christ Jesus. (Rom. 6:1–11)*

However, as with any religion, it is up to each individual to
practice what he believes. A lack of practice on the part of some
does not discredit the entire religion. Even for Islam, people do not
reject it because some members of the Nation of Islam assassinated
Malcolm X or because some Muslims are terrorists.

In terms of being practical, the Scriptures teach, "faith apart
from works is dead" (Jas. 2:26). Any faith in Christ that declares
one righteous before God will have works of righteousness that
follow. If you have seen people who claim to be Christian but do
not have lives that obey Scripture, you may not have been looking
at Christians at all.

In terms of visibility, who has not seen the church soup
kitchen, food pantry, clothing closet, or financial assistance given
to help those in need? How could anyone miss the church groups
that visit the jails, take food and blankets to the homeless, and have
activities to get young people off the street? Also, when it comes
to fighting for rights and justice for people of African descent in
America and around the world, it is the black church that has stood
out front, leading the way.

So if it is a credible, practical, visible religion you need, I commend the church to you. You need to get in there and be the person who lives like a Christian, stays rooted to the real lives and needs of people, and pushes your church to stand up for right in your community. And please do it in a hurry! Simon, Niger, Lucius, Augustine, Athanasius, Origen, Tertullian, and many others are waiting for you to step up and take your rightful place in history.

THINGS TO CONSIDER

1. Read again Acts 13:1–4. If men of African descent were part of the church from its earliest days, what does that say about Christianity being for black men, since Christianity preceded Islam by about six hundred years?
2. It is a good bet that someone near you practices the sort of sincere Christianity that you desire to see. Why not share with that person that you are reading this book and are looking to find real Christianity and the true church?
3. Pick up a good book that will give you an idea of how men like Augustine have contributed to the history of the world. I have one listed below. I think you will have pride about the black man's place in the church.

FOR FURTHER STUDY

Keener, Craig S. and Glenn Usry. *Defending Black Faith: Answers to Tough Questions about African-American Christianity.* Downers Grove, IL: InterVarsity Press, 1997.

Piper, John. *The Legacy of Sovereign Joy: God's Triumphant Grace in the Lives of Augustine, Luther, and Calvin.* Wheaton, IL: Crossway Books, 2000.

Shelly, Bruce L. *Church History in Plain Language*, 2nd edition. Nash-
    ville: Thomas Nelson, 1996.
Tsoukalas, Steven. *The Nation of Islam: Understanding Black Muslims*.
    Phillipsburg, NJ: P&R Publishing, 2001.
Usry, Glenn and Craig S. Keener. *Black Man's Religion: Can Christian-
    ity be Afrocentric?* Downers Grove, IL: InterVarsity Press, 1996.
Zacharias, Ravi. *Light in the Shadow of Jihad: The Struggle for Truth*.
    Sisters, OR: Multnomah, 2002.

And all who believed were together and had all things in common. And they were selling their possessions and belongings and distributing the proceeds to all, as any had need.

ACTS 2:44–45

Let the elders who rule well be considered worthy of double honor, especially those who labor in preaching and teaching. For the Scripture says, "You shall not muzzle an ox when it treads out the grain," and, "The laborer deserves his wages."

1 TIMOTHY 5:17–18

Now there is great gain in godliness with contentment, for we brought nothing into the world, and we cannot take anything out of the world. But if we have food and clothing, with these we will be content. But those who desire to be rich fall into temptation, into a snare, into many senseless and harmful desires that plunge people into ruin and destruction. For the love of money is a root of all kinds of evils. It is through this craving that some have wandered away from the faith and pierced themselves with many pangs.

1 TIMOTHY 6:6–10

AREN'T SOME CHURCHES JUST AFTER YOUR MONEY?

Some churches are just after your money, so it seems. This appears to be so obvious and prevalent that trying to convince you to go back to church without leaving your money at home is a definite challenge!

We all have seen the churches with huge, state-of-the-art buildings. We have been to a service where the offering plate has come around more than once, or where "tithers" are given recognition above others. In some experiences we have known people who have given the bulk of their livelihoods to a church, only to find out that the church was bilking them, and the leadership was financially corrupt. Then there is the persistent appearance that the preacher is getting rich off people, driving a luxury car, living in the best home in the suburbs or exurbia, and dressing himself and his wife in the finest clothes.

Your observations may have some validity. In the church there appears to be a great emphasis on giving money, and the trust of those who have charge of the money may be suspect. Why not offer a religion where money is rightly spoken of and where I can have assurance about what happens to my money once I give it? That is what you should expect—that people who claim to be holy are holy down to their wallets, purses, pockets, and offering plates, right? Please allow me to offer some comments on these common expectations.

1. You need to know that while some people overemphasize

1

money and giving in the church, no organized religion functions without money. Every building has utility bills that need to be paid, printing and educational material costs (for the Bible is not published for free, my friend), and staff salaries. The money needed to support these functions comes from those who give regularly to support them.

2. Money is mentioned in the Bible as part of church life. The members of the early church gave to support the work of those who preached the gospel and to support one another:

> And all who believed were together and had all things in common. And they were selling their possessions and belongings and distributing the proceeds to all, as any had need. (Acts 2:44–45)

They also took care of the poor, orphans, and widows. But their giving was never coached, demanded, or gained by acts of manipulation or intimidation. Instead people were encouraged to give cheerfully as they had means: "Each one must give as he has decided in his heart, not reluctantly or under compulsion, for God loves a cheerful giver" (2 Cor. 9:7). They gladly gave to see the work of the church continue, recognizing that the blessedness of giving excels the blessedness of receiving.

3. The church has a way of doing things collectively with money that an individual cannot accomplish with money. By pooling together funds collected by "tithes and offerings," some churches are able to offer before-care, aftercare, and tutoring after school to many neighborhood children. Families can receive crisis counseling, and some people can obtain job assistance.

4. The Bible teaches that faithful ministers of the gospel are to be supported financially by the people whom they serve (1 Cor. 9:1–15). In Scripture, the important work of the pastor and preacher is viewed as wage-deserving labor:

> *Let the elders who rule well be considered worthy of double honor, especially those who labor in preaching and teaching. For the Scripture says, "You shall not muzzle an ox when it treads out the grain," and, "The laborer deserves his wages." (1 Tim. 5:17–18)*

Those who benefit from instruction from the Word of God and the personal ministry of a pastor can in turn express thanks by supplying for the physical and material needs of the pastor from their collected giving.

As far as the show-off, cheat, and swindler are concerned, the early church also set a pattern for us to follow. Giving was never to be worn as a badge of boasting, but it was to be so spontaneous that the left hand would not know what the right hand was doing (Matt. 6:3). Offerings were always put into the hands of people who could be trusted, such as Titus (2 Cor. 8:16–24). Throughout the Bible, people who could not be trusted with money to be used for God's purposes, because of false motives or stealing, were frowned upon. Also, Scripture calls for ministers of the gospel to have the highest standards and the most pure motives toward money, including not being greedy for gain of money. All believers are to live contentedly within their means (1 Tim. 6:6–8). No one is to use God, the church, or the people of God to advance himself financially.

So, don't let your wallet keep you from going to church. You may give if you wish, but only if you can do so cheerfully and eagerly. If you do not trust those counting the money where you serve, privately ask the church's leadership where the money goes. If you do not like the verbal answer, ask to see a church budget, with the intent of giving to a ministry you have found to be financially responsible and faithful to the gospel. Then, if you live contentedly and give regularly to support what you know to be the work of God, you can be part of making a church that is after the good of people rather than their money. You can become one who will make sure that money given to the work of God goes where it is supposed to go.

THINGS TO CONSIDER

1. Think of how you spend your own money. Do you spend every cent without waste, debt, or extravagance, with perfect investment and savings of at least 10 percent of your income, and with an allowance to give to needy people without the expectation of anything in return? If someone were to scrutinize your financial stewardship the way a church's should be scrutinized, what would be found?
2. A good church tries to practice faithful stewardship of its money. If you were to become part of a good church with faithful stewardship, would you be prepared to give generously, as the Lord commands?

FOR FURTHER STUDY

Alcorn, Randy. *The Treasure Principle: Unlocking the Secret of Joyful Giving.* Sisters, OR: Multnomah, 2005.

Burkett, Larry. *Giving and Tithing.* Chicago: Moody, 1998.

Burkett, Larry. *How to Manage Your Money.* Chicago: Moody, 2002.

So whether we are at home or away, we make it our aim to please him. For we must all appear before the judgment seat of Christ, so that each one may receive what is due for what he has done in the body, whether good or evil.

2 CORINTHIANS 5:9–10

See to it that no one takes you captive by philosophy and empty deceit, according to human tradition, according to the elemental spirits of the world, and not according to Christ.

COLOSSIANS 2:8

And he gave the apostles, the prophets, the evangelists, the shepherds and teachers, to equip the saints for the work of ministry, for building up the body of Christ, until we all attain to the unity of the faith and of the knowledge of the Son of God, to mature manhood, to the measure of the stature of the fullness of Christ, so that we may no longer be children, tossed to and fro by the waves and carried about by every wind of doctrine, by human cunning, by craftiness in deceitful schemes.

EPHESIANS 4:11–14

IS ORGANIZED RELIGION NECESSARY?

You do not need organized religion to be religious. That is, you do not need religious practices guided by people and traditions of men to have a relationship with God. You feel you can go to God on your own, and each man's religion should be between himself and his Maker. Organized religion often produces fanatics and puts seemingly unnecessary measures of control on people. Also, you seem to be certain that God loves you, and you can talk to God whenever and however you want.

Let's face it. People have gone to their deaths trusting people who told them to forsake all and follow them. We all remember the Kool-Aid in Jonestown, the UFOs in San Diego, and the fires in Waco. People who promoted colonization of Africa and killed in the Crusades and Inquisition all did so in the name of organized religion. Some people leave family at the prompting of religion, while others stop all common forms of leisure and recreational contact with the world in the name of organized religion. Many suicide bombers in the Middle East are hoping to be righteous martyrs in the cause of organized religion. Not to mention, there are all those rules and rituals you remember from childhood: no drinking, no playing cards, no makeup, no "worldly" music or dancing, and church all day on Sunday—your only real day off!

I am willing to bet that if you could have a relationship with God without unnecessary burdens, you would find church—

organized religion—to be enjoyable and desirable. But first let me say this: organized religion should seem just as natural as the rest of your organized life. What do I mean?

You probably do not have an unorganized occupation. While you could do your job on your own, you would not be a productive member of society apart from your company's organizational structure, marketing, management, and human resource department. In fact, you would never get a paycheck without organization. Even if you were self-employed this would be true, for you must at least be organized enough to keep records, pay bills, pay taxes, and pay yourself and your employees. Your work environment also has a code of conduct in order to protect its employees and the reputation of a company's workplace.

More than likely, you have not experienced unorganized education. You may have experienced poorly organized education, but never unorganized education. Even if you claim to be self-educated from kindergarten through college, you followed a curriculum and gave a record of your learning to a local government education agency. You kept records, followed a schedule, and matriculated according to a sequence. If publicly educated, you were part of a structure of teachers, administrators, food service workers, security personnel, coaches, bus drivers, and maintenance workers. Without the input of each of them, you could not have been educated. If you were home-educated, a parent or group of parents played these roles. While going through school, you had to meet your state's standards for the minimum content of education necessary to graduate.

You probably would not like unorganized health care. At some point you would need more than home remedies, a first-aid kit, and two aspirin. Then you would go to see a doctor. But who schedules your appointment if there is no organization? Who keeps a record of each visit? How does your doctor become educated enough to give you an accurate diagnosis or to tell you if you are improving in your health? Who would give you a clean bed in the hospital, supply your medicines, send up those trays with mildly seasoned food, and wash your soiled gown—the one with the back out? What would you do without pharmaceutical regulations to prevent the wrong mixes of medicine or to keep you from obtaining as many painkillers as you like but may not actually need?

Do I need to question your experience with unorganized law, unorganized government, unorganized family, or unorganized auto care? You get the picture. Organized institutions and industries offer far greater benefits and protection, and less confusion, than unorganized institutions or equivalents.

Unorganized religion would work the same way as other unorganized institutions. Or, to turn the images around, organized religion—speaking now only for the church—intends the good of every individual. The organizational structure of the church is for the joy of all people in the church: "Obey your leaders and submit to them, for they are keeping watch over your souls, as those who will have to give an account. Let them do this with joy and not with groaning, for that would be of no advantage to you" (Heb. 13:17). The organizational structure ensures that an educational program to learn about God can be offered (for no one who has found the truth has ever studied to know God completely on his own). Organization allows for growth to be measured and for orderly Sunday services to take place. When you have completely spontaneous religion—i.e., unorganized—services seem to be a hodgepodge of religious acts that run for many hours. Organization is necessary to make sure the church stays on purpose for the task to which it is called, and organization is supposed to keep radicals and fanatics from destroying the church.

But more importantly, the church, though it has organization, functions primarily like a living organism and a family. It is a group of people, called by God to Jesus Christ, who are as interdependent as human body parts. It is also a family of brothers and sisters who are to love one another and consider the needs of others more than each of their own individual needs. Organization allows the organism to function properly. The organism keeps the organization from becoming a place of rigidity, lacking love, grace, and mercy.

Most importantly, the church makes claim to a personal relationship. That is, the church is made up of people who day by day relate to God as Father, Judge, Savior, Mediator, Advocate, and Lord. Through prayer we talk to God about our needs. Through his Word, he speaks to us to tell us his will and to give us his joy. Through worship we express the greatness of his worth to us.

In confession we tell the Lord how we have failed in our relationship with him. In evangelism we tell others that this relationship is like no other—just as we would if we found the earthly love of our lives! Those who personally relate to God the Father and Jesus the Savior organize themselves into a great happy family in order to celebrate God, learn about him, and tell others about him. I invite you to drop all thoughts of any other religion, for only Christianity—the church—can offer you a personal relationship with God through his Son, Jesus Christ. If you accept that offer, you will see that the church is a living, breathing, loving relationship, organized but not rigidly religious. Won't you accept that invitation to be part of the church? To help you, let us clear one more hurdle in the next chapter.

THINGS TO CONSIDER

1. Think of an organization to which you have belonged. If you had said, "I want to define the purpose and goals of this group without anyone else's input, leadership, direction, or help," how would your experience have differed?
2. What would you think of a religious group that claimed to be following God but had absolutely no rules, guidelines, leadership, or structure to guide its members toward a goal?
3. God has laid out a plan in the Scriptures for the organization of the church, and God has laid out a plan for that organized church to reach everyone with the good news of salvation through his Son, Jesus Christ. What might such foresight on God's part say about his concern for reaching you and filling your life with joy?

FOR FURTHER STUDY

Piper, John. *Desiring God: Meditations of a Christian Hedonist*. Sisters, OR: Multnomah, 2003.

Ridenour, Fritz. *So What's the Difference?* Ventura, CA: Regal Books/ Gospel Light, 2001.

And Jesus said, "I am, and you will see the Son of Man seated at the right hand of Power, and coming with the clouds of heaven." And the high priest tore his garments and said, "What further witnesses do we need? You have heard his blasphemy. What is your decision?" And they all condemned him as deserving death.

MARK 14:62–64

And this was why the Jews were persecuting Jesus, because he was doing these things on the Sabbath. But Jesus answered them, "My Father is working until now, and I am working." This was why the Jews were seeking all the more to kill him, because not only was he breaking the Sabbath, but he was even calling God his own Father, making himself equal with God.

JOHN 5:16–18

JESUS NEVER CLAIMED TO BE GOD, DID HE?

I cannot outright give you the high-five on this one. I know that Islam claims Jesus was a prophet. I am aware that others claim that he was a great teacher and that his teachings are on par with or above those of other great religious men. It is true that the Bible does not contain one statement in which Jesus said, "I am God" in those exact words. You may feel that his followers later elevated him to the status of deity.

However, the Bible, with great clarity, reveals the identity of Jesus Christ.

• Though Jesus never said the words, "I am God," he did say other words that could only be said by one who is God, such as, "The Father judges no one, but has given all judgment to the Son, that all may honor the Son, just as they honor the Father. Whoever does not honor the Son does not honor the Father who sent him," and "I and the Father are one" (John 5:22–23; 10:30). In order to say that the Father is not honored when the Son is not honored, the Son must have a status equal to that of the Father. Otherwise, it would be entirely possible to dishonor the Son, yet still honor the Father. Jesus is making a statement about his deity. That Jesus claimed to be God is confirmed by the charges of blasphemy from Jewish leaders (John 5:18; 10:31–33).

• Though Jesus never said, "I am God," he did make other "I am" statements that were intended to say, "I am God," such as "I am the bread of life; whoever comes to me shall not hunger, and whoever believes in me shall never thirst," and "I am the resurrection and the life" (John 6:35; 11:25). Jesus offers himself as bread that is eternally satisfying, filling all spiritual hunger. Jesus also offers himself as the very one in whom the resurrection from the dead, and the obtaining of eternal life, is embodied. That is, if anyone will be raised from the dead to enjoy God's presence forever, that person will be raised because of Jesus' resurrection and work on the cross alone. Only God could make such statements.

• Though Jesus never said, "I am God," Jesus received worship as God. Jesus never said, "Do not worship me, for I am not God" (see Matthew 14:33; 28:9; Luke 24:52; John 9:38; Acts 10:25; cf. Matt. 4:8–10; Rev. 22:8–9). This separates him from angels, who also worship Jesus as if he were God (Heb. 1:1–14). This separates him from mere humans, whom the Bible forbids us to worship.

• Though Jesus never said, "I am God," he said and did things God says and does. In Mark 2 a paralytic was lowered through the roof of a house. When Jesus saw the faith of the friends of the paralytic, he said, "your sins are forgiven" (v. 5). Those around him quickly recognized that Jesus was taking a prerogative that belongs to God alone. Rather than denying his right to this prerogative, Jesus demonstrated that he has the power to forgive sins by healing the paralytic. Jesus thereby made a claim to be God by his words and actions.

• Though Jesus never said, "I am God," he was proclaimed to be God by his followers, and never stopped them from saying he is God. Thomas recognized Christ as God after the resurrection, saying, "My

Lord and my God!" (John 20:28). The apostle John, identifying Jesus Christ as "the Word," says, "the Word was God" (John 1:1).

So then Jesus is clearly portrayed to be God in the Scriptures. Recognizing this, C. S. Lewis made this insightful conclusion:

> I am trying here to prevent anyone saying the really foolish thing that people often say about Him: "I'm ready to accept Jesus as a great moral teacher, but I don't accept His claim to be God." That is one thing we must not say. A man who was merely a man and said the sort of things Jesus said would not be a great moral teacher. He would either be a lunatic—on the level with a man who says he is a poached egg—or he would be the Devil of Hell. You must take your choice. Either this was, and is, the Son of God: or else a madman or something worse. You can shut Him up for a fool, you can spit at Him and kill Him as a demon; or you can fall at His feet and call Him Lord and God. But let us not come with any patronizing nonsense about His being a great human teacher. He has not left that open to us. He did not intend to.[1]

But whether or not Jesus claimed expressly to be God in those exact words is not really the problem. The problem is this: if Jesus Christ is God, then in rejecting a personal relationship with him, you are rejecting a personal relationship with God, and the only way to life. This issue is whether you will submit to him as God and Lord. Please know this:

• Only God could devise a satisfying plan to solve his just demands. God demands absolute holiness, perfection, and righteousness for a person to stand in his presence. All people fail to meet this standard because "all have sinned and fall short of the glory of God" (Rom. 3:23). To sin is to miss the mark of God's standard, to break the law of God, or to disregard the law of God. Everyone has done this daily in life, whether the sin is lying, showing favoritism, ignoring the plight of the needy, or thinking more highly of oneself than one ought. If you are not convinced that you sin daily, consider that you did disobey your parents at least once in life, which keeps you from meeting God's standard of holiness. And when that holy standard is missed, God requires the death of the sinner and wrath against sin in order to meet his righteous requirement of holiness: "The wages of sin is death"; "because of your hard and impenitent heart you are storing up wrath for yourself on the day of wrath when God's righteous judgment will be revealed" (Rom. 6:23; 2:5).

• Only God could defeat death so that he could offer life. God, seeing mankind's dilemma, sent his Son, Jesus Christ, into the world. God the Son took on human likeness as a man, lived among men, and kept God's law perfectly from birth to death. Being perfect, he qualified to meet the demands of God for man to be righteous before God. But God still required payment for sin in order for his justice to be carried out: man must die for his sin and suffer the wrath of God. But God presented his Son, Jesus Christ, as a man, to die in place of mankind and to suffer the wrath of God:

> For all have sinned and fall short of the glory of God, and are justified by his grace as a gift, through the redemption that is in Christ Jesus, whom God put forward as a propitiation by his blood, to be received by faith. This was to show God's righteousness, because in his divine forbearance he had passed

over former sins. It was to show his righteousness at the present time, so that he might be just and the justifier of the one who has faith in Jesus. (Rom. 3:23–26)

After living a perfect life, Jesus died on the cross as a substitute for all people and their sins. Three days later Jesus rose from the dead. This demonstrates that Jesus has power over death, for death could not hold him in the grave. If he has power over death, then he can also keep death from holding down anyone he chooses. He can offer life after death—eternal life—to anyone who will turn from sin and believe his death and resurrection to be sufficient payment for sin and power for eternal life.

Your last hurdle for not going to church, that Jesus never specifically claimed to be God, is really saying that if Jesus did in fact lay claim to be God, then you would follow him. Indeed, he very much claimed to be God—the one true God, and the only way to God and eternal life.

You may not want to go to church, but you cannot afford to ignore Christ as Savior and Lord. On this one you will only be right if you turn from sin and trust in him.

THINGS TO CONSIDER

Consider again Romans 3:23–26. God put to death his very own Son in order to offer you life. But those who have not trusted in his Son Jesus remain in their sins and under the wrath of God. Examine your life and see if you are prepared to meet with God. If not, plead with him for mercy, asking him to forgive you of your sins based on the death and resurrection of his Son. Place your trust in Jesus Christ alone for eternal life.

FOR FURTHER STUDY

Beisner, E. Calvin. *Answers for Atheists, Agnostics, and Other Thoughtful Skeptics: Dialogs about Christian Faith and Life*. Wheaton, IL: Crossway Books, 1993.

Geisler, Norman and Frank Turek. *I Don't Have Enough Faith to Be an Atheist*. Wheaton, IL: Crossway Books, 2004.

Stott, John. *Why I Am a Christian*. Downers Grove, IL: InterVarsity Press, 2004.

NOTE

[1] C. S. Lewis, *Mere Christianity* (New York: Macmillan, 1960), 55–56.

Pay careful attention to yourselves and to all the flock,
in which the Holy Spirit has made you overseers,
to care for the church of God, which he obtained with
his own blood. I know that after my departure fierce
wolves will come in among you, not sparing the flock;
and from among your own selves will arise men
speaking twisted things, to draw away
the disciples after them.

ACTS 20:28–30

Of this gospel I was made a minister according to the
gift of God's grace, which was given me by the
working of his power. To me, though I am the very least
of all the saints, this grace was given, to preach to the
Gentiles the unsearchable riches of Christ, and to bring
to light for everyone what is the plan of the mystery
hidden for ages in God who created all things,
so that through the church the manifold wisdom of God
might now be made known to the rulers and
authorities in the heavenly places.

EPHESIANS 3:7-10

WHAT TO LOOK FOR TO FIND A GOOD CHURCH

When you finally do get to visit a church, in order to evaluate whether this church is healthy and good for you, please consider asking that church the following questions:

1. *Gospel*. Does this church believe and teach that Jesus Christ, God the Son, alone provides salvation through his death and resurrection to whom he will, whoever calls on his name in faith, apart from works on the part of man?

2. *Worship*. Does this church command its members to passionately pursue God together with thanksgiving, praise, song, confession, and the celebration of the Lord's Supper? Does it command worship of God the Father and God the Son (by means of God the Holy Spirit) alone, without the mixture of worship or exaltation of any other human or divine figure?

3. *Preaching*. Does this church emphasize the preaching of the Word of God in its entirety, with explanation of the Scriptures as described in Chapter 4? Does the preaching exalt God and his Son, Jesus Christ, as the greatest beauty in life, the only answer to the plight of mankind, and the centerpiece and unifying idea of all Scripture and history?

4. *Teaching*. Does this church have a statement of what it teaches that is consistent with the teaching of the church throughout history? Such a document may be called a statement of doctrine or a statement of faith. It is a statement indicating that the truth of

God's Word is of utmost importance to this church. Sample statements to which to compare this church's statement may be:

- The Westminster Confession of Faith
  (http://www.reformed.org/documents/index_docu.html)
- The Baptist Faith and Message 2000
  (http://www.sbc.net/bfm/bfm2000.asp)
- Confessional Statement of The Gospel Coalition
  (http://thegospelcoalition.org/confessionalstatement.php)

It is also important to ask questions concerning a church's views about gender and the family. See the Danvers Statement of the Council for Biblical Manhood and Womanhood for help in evaluating standards of Christian truth on gender and family (http://www.cbmw.org/Danvers). In addition, does this church provide times in which members can learn the Scriptures, doctrine, and moral standards, so that its members can grow in the Christian faith?

5. *Prayer.* Do the members of this church gather to pray to the Lord, and is prayer emphasized as the means to receive the power of God to live uprightly before him?

6. *Evangelism.* Does this church emphasize seeking the salvation of people from the wrath of God by engaging people with the gospel?

7. *Love.* Does there seem to be a sense of love, care, kindness, and concern for all of the members, regardless of the life status of the members? Does this church seem to show care for its hurting and needy members?

8. *Holiness.* Does this church have moral standards for its members? Such standards may often be found in a church cov-

enant. Does this church have a means for addressing sin and disobedience among its members and a process of restoring those who have fallen away from the church but wish to return?

THINGS TO CONSIDER

1. Looking for a good church can be hard work. It will take patience. Plan to take at least two or three Sundays in a row to visit one church. You can learn more about a church the more Sundays you attend. You can learn even more if you attend one of that church's services during the week, or its Sunday evening service, for a few weeks in a row. Also consider attending a church's new members' class or equivalent, without feeling obligated to remain at that church. In this way you can get the best assessment of a church.

2. Many people feel locked into attending the church they have attended most of their lives, whether that be a church of a particular denomination, a particular location, or one's family relations. However, you are not bound to attend a church simply because of a past relationship with that church. If a church is not what the church is called to be and do, then attending such a church will only serve to reinforce a negative idea of church. I encourage you to find a good church by looking past the music and the numbers of people in attendance to its main worship services. The church is too important to your life for you to simply settle for a church because it is convenient to you.

FOR FURTHER STUDY

Dever, Mark. *Nine Marks of a Healthy Church*. Wheaton, IL: Crossway Books, 2004.

Harris, Joshua. *Stop Dating the Church! Fall in Love with the Family of God*. Sisters, OR: Multnomah, 2004.

"For the Son of Man is going to come with his angels in the glory of his Father, and then he will repay each person according to what he has done."

MATTHEW 16:27

"But in those days, after that tribulation, the sun will be darkened, and the moon will not give its light, and the stars will be falling from heaven, and the powers in the heavens will be shaken. And then they will see the Son of Man coming in clouds with great power and glory. And then he will send out the angels and gather his elect from the four winds, from the ends of the earth to the ends of heaven."

MARK 13:24–27

Then comes the end, when he delivers the kingdom to God the Father after destroying every rule and every authority and power. For he must reign until he has put all his enemies under his feet.

1 CORINTHIANS 15:24–25

THE FULFILLMENT OF OLD TESTAMENT PROPHECIES ABOUT CHRIST IN THE NEW TESTAMENT

The Bible is a book with two main sections—the Old Testament and the New Testament. The Old Testament's last book was written five hundred years before the first New Testament book was written. The Old Testament's last book was written more than four hundred years before the birth of Christ. Therefore, if someone in the Old Testament wrote something about Jesus Christ, he did so without personally knowing Christ and without being present to witness the events of which he spoke. Such writings are identified as prophecy, for they foretell of the life of Christ.

Several Old Testament passages speak about Christ's ministry on the earth. Many times the New Testament writers refer to these prophecies when speaking about the life of Jesus Christ. Only a few of them need to be examined to see that the Bible is indeed unique in its ability to present specific, verifiable prophecies with 100 percent accuracy.

1. *Jesus' birth*. The Gospel of Matthew records that Jesus' mother was pregnant before the man she was to marry ever had relations with her (Matt. 1:18–25). The passage assumes her virginity, for an immoral woman in Israel was to be stoned to death. But the story tells us that an angel spoke to Joseph about Christ, saying, "that which is conceived in her is from the Holy Spirit." Matthew then

says, "All this took place to fulfill what the Lord had spoken by the prophet: 'Behold, the virgin shall conceive and bear a son, and they shall call his name Immanuel' (which means, God with us)." The prophet that Matthew quotes is Isaiah, who gave this prophecy in the eighth century B.C. (see Isa. 7:14). Note that Isaiah and Matthew are both specific about his birth to a virgin, not simply to a woman.

2. *Jesus' entry into Jerusalem.* When Jesus enters the city of Jerusalem to be received as King of the Jews, he comes riding on a donkey. We could speculate about the other means by which Jesus could have come into the city, including walking or by camel (Mark 10:25), suggesting that coming on a donkey is unique. However, Matthew draws out the uniqueness of this event with these words:

> *This took place to fulfill what was spoken by the prophet, saying, "Say to the daughter of Zion, 'Behold, your king is coming to you, humble, and mounted on a donkey, and on a colt, the foal of a beast of burden.'" (21:4–5)*

Matthew recognizes that the prophet Zechariah spoke of this event in the sixth century B.C., more than six hundred years before Christ rode into Jerusalem. The accuracy of Zechariah's words and the fulfillment in Matthew can be seen in that both the donkey and colt were spoken of as part of Jesus' entry into Jerusalem. While a donkey may have been a common animal providing a coincidental happening, the specificity of a donkey and its colt, both in the prophecy and in the fulfillment, makes the possibility of coincidence unlikely.

3. *Jesus' death and resurrection.* As the central event of all Scripture and history, the Bible repeatedly speaks of Christ's death and also of his resurrection. The New Testament writers indicate in multiple places that the events around Jesus' death and resurrection fulfilled Old Testament prophecies:

Event	Old Testament Prophecy	New Testament Fulfillment
His trial and mocking	**Ps. 22:18:** They divide my garments among them, and for my clothing they cast lots.	**John 19:24:** So they said to one another, "Let us not tear it, but cast lots for it to see whose it shall be." This was to fulfill the Scripture which says, "They divided my garments among them, and for my clothing they cast lots."
His crucifixion	**Zech. 12:10:** When they look on me, on him whom they have pierced, they shall mourn for him, as one mourns for an only child.	**John 19:37:** And again another Scripture says, "They will look on him whom they have pierced."
His resurrection	**Ps. 16:10:** For you will not abandon my soul to Sheol, or let your holy one see corruption.	**Acts 2:25–27:** For David says concerning him . . . "For you will not abandon my soul to Hades, or let your Holy One see corruption."

Events such as the tearing of Jesus' garment, the piercing of his side, and his resurrection are specific enough to speak of fulfillment, not of coincidence. Even so, these examples are only a handful of the more than four hundred Old Testament prophecies that speak about Christ and are fulfilled exactly as prophesied in the New Testament record of the life of Christ. If these were coincidences, the Bible would still be an amazing book about one man who had more coincidences between his life and the word of people who lived four hundred to twelve hundred years before him than any other person known to mankind! But these are not coincidences. These are the accurate words of men who spoke for God prior to the birth of Christ. You would do well to put your trust in the book that records their words and the life of the Son of God on the earth.

THINGS TO CONSIDER

1. Consider the prophecies of Christ in the Old Testament and their fulfillment. God spoke these words hundreds of years before they came to be. And when they came to be, they were fulfilled with 100 percent accuracy. What might that say about the reliability of the rest of the Word of God?
2. One of the things prophesied in the New Testament is the return of Jesus Christ to claim those who love him, to establish his final rule, and to cast his enemies into the Lake of Fire (see the verses at the beginning of this chapter). Considering the accuracy of all of the other prophecies in Scripture, if the prophecies about Christ's return are equally accurate, what does that say about your fate when he returns?

FOR FURTHER STUDY

Clowney, Edmund. *The Unfolding Mystery: Discovering Christ in the Old Testament.* Phillipsburg, NJ: P&R, 1991.

Dever, Mark. *The Message of the New Testament: Promises Kept.*
    Wheaton, IL: Crossway Books, 2005.

Goldsworthy, Graeme. *According to Plan: The Unfolding Revelation of
    God in the Bible.* Downers Grove, IL: InterVarsity Press, 2002.

White, James. *Scripture Alone: Exploring the Bible's Accuracy, Author-
    ity, and Authenticity.* Minneapolis: Bethany, 2004.

Therefore God gave them up in the lusts of their hearts to impurity, to the dishonoring of their bodies among themselves, because they exchanged the truth about God for a lie and worshiped and served the creature rather than the Creator, who is blessed forever! Amen. For this reason God gave them up to dishonorable passions. For their women exchanged natural relations for those that are contrary to nature; and the men likewise gave up natural relations with women and were consumed with passion for one another, men committing shameless acts with men and receiving in themselves the due penalty for their error.

ROMANS 1:24–27

And the angels who did not stay within their own position of authority, but left their proper dwelling, he has kept in eternal chains under gloomy darkness until the judgment of the great day—just as Sodom and Gomorrah and the surrounding cities, which likewise indulged in sexual immorality and pursued unnatural desire, serve as an example by undergoing a punishment of eternal fire.

JUDE 6–7

THE CHURCH DOES NOT WELCOME HOMOSEXUALS

From where you sit, it seems that the church does not readily welcome homosexuals. This idea exists in spite of the fact that we play and sing music written by James Cleveland, we quote the poetry of James Baldwin in our sermons, and we dress in outfits designed by Willie Smith. The church's hesitancy to embrace homosexuals continues despite the fact that much of the music produced, sung, and directed in the church is done by homosexuals. The rejection continues even though some very well-known ministers have admitted to being bisexual or homosexual. In addition, we know that there is an underworld in which African-American leaders are living a double lifestyle on the down-low.

Some members of the African-American community are homosexual. Many of the people in our community who are dying from HIV/AIDS have had homosexual relationships. Mainstream culture, including mainstream African-American culture, is opening its arms to people with different sexual orientations. It seems, therefore, that the church is out of touch with the times, hypocritical in its message about the love of God, or at the very least homophobic.

Yes, we are guilty. We, the church, do not readily embrace homosexuals with outstretched arms. Truthfully, some churches will not even accept a "don't ask, don't tell" policy (see Day 3). We are in contradiction with mainstream culture. We have a problem with saying one can believe on Jesus and be a homosexual. We appear to be talking out of both sides of our mouths when on the one hand we say, "God loves you" and "love your neighbor as yourself," but on the other hand appear to say, "Such love does not welcome homosexuals into the family of God."

As a pastor who has buried homosexuals (and those who have died from HIV/AIDS due to homosexual relationships) and who cares for his church members who have loved ones who are homosexual, I am familiar with your concern. I also know that many so-called Christians and churchgoers have made hateful actions against homosexuals and have said many vicious, vile, and harmful things toward homosexuals that do not reflect God's love for people made in his image. Nor do they reflect the grace, love, and kindness of the Christ who received lepers, accepted worship from prostitutes, dialogued with a Samaritan woman at a well, told the story of the prodigal son, selected a tax-collector to be included among his disciples, and ate dinner at the home of Zacchaeus. Moreover, Jesus welcomed into his kingdom the thief on the cross, one guilty of capital theft. In fact, it seems that Jesus expressed greater concern with the self-righteousness of the religious establishment of his day than with the sinfulness of those portrayed as society's sinful. How then should we look at the church's rejection of homosexuals?

First, let us be truthful about one thing: it is only recently that homosexuals are being readily accepted as part of mainstream African-American culture. In current attempts to revise African-American history, some people appeal to the exceptions, like the boldness of James Baldwin and the reception of Johnny Mathis by all audiences, in order to argue that homosexuality always existed as a norm within our community and American society. However, as late as 1984, in the movie *Revenge of the Nerds*, the actor cast as the African-American nerd was portrayed as a homosexual. To the filmmakers, for an African-American to be homosexual was deviant from the norm for mainstream African-American life; it was nerdy, not normal. If there is any measure of values, attitude, and atmosphere of "mainstream" culture, certainly Hollywood acts as the barometer. In the case of homosexuality, the barometer was still low in favor of acceptance among African-Americans in the mid-1980s. Even in 1993 Denzel Washington was cast as a homophobic lawyer in the movie *Philadelphia*. As an African-American lawyer, he did not readily embrace homosexuality, and neither did our community in the early 1990s as represented by Washington's character.

Second, the reality of homosexuality in the church does not mean it should be acceptable, if it can be shown that homosexuality violates the teachings of the Word of God. In reality, many clergymen have been found guilty of embezzlement, adultery, plagiarism, and pedophilia. Surely this does not mean that these crimes and sins should be viewed as acceptable by the church? If this were true, what would make the church distinct from the rest of society? Not to mention, what trust would you put in the preaching and practice of a congregation full of unashamed embezzlers, adulterers, plagiarizers, and pedophiles? Would you put your money in its offering plate? Would you allow your spouse to attend any of its functions alone? Would you believe that the minister had heard from God or think he had merely borrowed from someone else? Would you send your child to children's church? Would you believe that church's message about God's power to change your life when it could not change the lives of these criminals who claim to be following the message? Would you accuse someone of having embezzlephobia for not readily embracing practicing embezzlers as church members?

Now you could reply, "That's not fair! Those items you mentioned are crimes. Homosexual acts between consenting adults are not illegal." This is true, although it has only been legally true since the 2003 ruling in *Lawrence v. Texas*, in which the Texas statute forbidding two persons of the same sex to engage in intimate sexual conduct was ruled unconstitutional. Nevertheless, I mentioned the above crimes because they are sins. I did this so that you might understand that the issue of rejection of homosexuals by the church is a matter of a lifestyle of sin, not a matter of homophobia or hypocrisy.

This brings us to a third significant truth: the Bible identifies homosexuality as sin. *Sin* is missing God's standard for holiness and thus missing the ability to have a relationship with God, for he is absolutely perfect in holiness. Homosexuality is an act that misses God's standard for holiness, as seen in 1 Corinthians 6:9–11:

> *Or do you not know that the unrighteous will not inherit the kingdom of God? Do not be deceived: neither the sexually immoral, nor idolaters, nor adulterers, nor men who practice homosexuality, nor thieves, nor the greedy, nor drunkards, nor revilers, nor swindlers will inherit the kingdom of God. And such were some of you. But you were washed, you were sancti-*

fied, you were justified in the name of the Lord Jesus Christ and by the Spirit of our God. (also see Gal. 5:19–21 and 1 Tim. 1:8–11)

Homosexual persons are labeled as "unrighteous," as those who "will not inherit the kingdom of God." Moreover, these verses indicate that the practice of homosexuality is a behavior with which Christians have made a clean break by being "washed" (cleansed from sin by God), "sanctified" (set apart from sin for God), and "justified" (declared righteous in the sight of God) by Jesus Christ and the Holy Spirit. Homosexuality and following Christ are not compatible.

Moreover, homosexual practice and church membership cannot coexist if the church is to remain free of evil, as seen in 1 Corinthians 5:9–13:

I wrote to you in my letter not to associate with sexually immoral people—not at all meaning the sexually immoral of this world, or the greedy and swindlers, or idolaters, since then you would need to go out of the world. But now I am writing to you not to associate with anyone who bears the name of brother if he is guilty of sexual immorality or greed, or is an idolater, reviler, drunkard, or swindler—not even to eat with such a one. For what have I to do with judging outsiders? Is it not those inside the church whom you are to judge? God judges those outside. "Purge the evil person from among you." (also see Eph. 5:5–8)

Christians, like those in the Corinthian church, have the responsibility "not to associate with sexually immoral people" who claim to be "brothers" in the faith, and this includes homosexuals. Instead each church has the responsibility to remove from its congregation those in a lifestyle of sin. Those with homosexual behavior may be received into the church only after a profession of Christ that is accompanied by a complete break—repentance—from a lifestyle of homosexuality.

Yet it remains true that Jesus received people with sinful lifestyles. I cited several examples above. Let us look at each of these examples:

• When a leper approached Jesus, Jesus reached out his hand and touched him in spite of the outcast status of the leper. However, the Scriptures first record the leper saying, "Lord, if you will, you can make me clean" (Matt. 8:2; Mark 1:40; Luke 5:12). The leper recognized the deity of Christ, his sovereign freedom to cleanse or not cleanse, and his full ability to make the leper clean. The leper was not asking Jesus to accept him as a leper and allow him to continue in his leprosy. He was asking the sovereign God to change his life. In fact, the accounts in Mark and Luke indicate that the leper pleaded with Jesus to cleanse him. While having leprosy itself was not a sin, having leprosy did place one in a position in which healing was needed before the (former) leper could approach God. Similarly, the ten lepers cried, "Jesus, Master, have mercy on us." They, too, recognized Christ as master of their lives and their need for mercy from him. In fact, the one who gave thanks for his cleansing was told, "your faith has made you well" (Luke 17:11–19).

• One of the prostitutes who was received by Jesus in the home of a religious leader heard Jesus say, "your sins are forgiven." As a result, "[her] faith saved [her]" from the penalty due her sins. The account of the demonstration of her faith says:

> *And behold, a woman of the city, who was a sinner, when she learned that he was reclining at table in the Pharisee's house, brought an alabaster flask of ointment, and standing behind him at his feet, weeping, she began to wet his feet with her tears and wiped them with the hair of her head and kissed his feet and anointed them with the ointment. (Luke 7:37–38, 48)*

The woman, in humility toward Christ, did not face him directly but stood behind him so as not to look as if she were propositioning him. She took ointment for her occupation and used it to honor the Christ instead of using it to allure Christ. She poured out tears of remorse, used her own hair as a towel, and demonstrated homage to him by kissing his feet (rather than attempting to kiss him in an erotic manner). The woman recognized him as Lord—the one who could forgive her sins. She did not expect him to allow her to remain as a prostitute. Furthermore, Jesus says that this was evidence of her "love" for the one whom she sought to forgive her sins (v. 47). Her love was not indicated by the "love" she offered on the street to men. Her love toward him came with shame for sin and a change in lifestyle.

• Jesus had a conversation with the Samaritan woman at the well with full knowledge that she was an adulterer. Jesus confronted this woman's sins in a conversation that led her to recognize him as the Messiah. He did not leave her as simply a Samaritan but led her to acknowledge the Jewish man confronting her as the Savior of all people in the world (John 4:1–42).

• When Jesus called Levi to himself, he called him to "follow me." Levi (aka Matthew) responded by "leaving everything," including the money he made from cheating the people, indicating he was leaving his former ways (Luke 5:27–28). Later, while at Levi's house eating with other tax collectors, Jesus informed the religious leaders that he had come "to call . . . sinners to repentance" (v. 32). He called Levi, Levi turned from his sinful way to Christ, and he left his sin as he followed Jesus as a disciple. Similarly Zacchaeus the tax collector, finding out who Jesus is, gave half of his riches to the poor and promised to pay 400 percent of what was stolen from each person from whom he had collected taxes. Zacchaeus made a change of life when he met Jesus (Luke 19:1–8).

• In the case of the thief on the cross next to Jesus' cross, the thief was fearful of confronting God as a thief. Rebuking the other thief for ridiculing Jesus, he recognized Jesus as the Jewish King, asking Jesus to remember him when he arrived in his kingdom:

> One of the criminals who were hanged railed at him, saying, "Are you not the Christ? Save yourself and us!" But the other rebuked him, saying, "Do you not fear God, since you are under the same sentence of condemnation? And we indeed justly, for we are receiving the due reward of our deeds; but this man has done nothing wrong." And he said, "Jesus, remember me when you come into your kingdom." And he said to him, "Truly, I say to you, today you will be with me in Paradise." (Luke 23:39–43)

The thief fully recognized that Jesus, on the other side of death, would be King in the kingdom he had been preaching. He also recognized Jesus' ability to bring him into that kingdom. In effect, he asked the King to pardon him for his sins rather than mocking the King in his sinfulness (Luke 23:32–42). The thief's repentance is evident from his apparent change in heart. He could not continue in the mocking of Jesus that he had been practicing with the other thief (Matt. 27:44; Mark 15:32). Jesus was able to assure the thief of acceptance in his kingdom because the thief had repented from sin and trusted Jesus for his salvation.

• In the case of the prodigal son (Luke 15:11–32), in which the prodigal represents the sinner and the father represents God, the prodigal did not expect the father to express forgiveness. But when the son turned from his wasteful lifestyle, he then returned home and was welcomed into the house by his father. For the prodigal, repentance from sin preceded acceptance by the father.

In summary, each person was received by Jesus as he or she 1) recognized him as Lord, 2) repented of his or her past—turned away from the previous lifestyles, 3) expressed faith in him for salvation from his or her past way of living, and 4) demonstrated change from his or her past and accepted the standards for following Jesus. Initial reception of each sinner became ongoing acceptance only after a change of lifestyle by faith in Christ on the part of those practicing sin. The modern concept of "come as you are," flaunting and justifying one's sinful inclinations without thought of seeking a change in lifestyle, differs from the description of Jesus' encounter with sinners in the Gospels. For Jesus, "come as you are" meant to come to him and be readily welcomed by him in one's sinful identity. But it also meant coming to him in brokenness over one's sin, seeking to be changed from that identity in order for there to be ongoing acceptance from him (i.e., salvation). Even the account of the woman caught in adultery depicts the woman's recognition of Jesus as "Lord" and Jesus' demands for the woman to change her adulterous ways: "go, and from now on sin no more" (John 8:1–11).[1]

This type of reception of sinners was not limited to Jesus' earthly ministry: this was the message preached by his disciples as they preached to people to "repent and turn to God, performing deeds in keeping with their repentance" (Acts 26:20; see also 5:31; 8:22; 17:30; 20:21). This finds agreement in the epistles' expectation that all people "should reach repentance" (2 Pet. 3:9; see also Rom. 2:4; 1 Thess. 1:9; 2 Tim. 2:25; Heb. 6:6). Therefore, in order to be faithful to the Scriptures, the final authority for faith and practice as a Christian, the church must call homosexuality sin, reject from membership those who do not change from a sinful lifestyle, and yet receive those who desire to turn from homosexuality and any other sinful lifestyle.

Therefore, if your homosexuality is the concern keeping you from church, go to church and observe the worship. You should be welcomed into the public worship service. Expect to hear that the Lord will rescue you from his judgment upon sin, give you the power to resist fulfillment of homosexual desires, and grant you the joy of life as a heterosexual in a monogamous marital relationship of fidelity or in joy as a single in contentment and holiness.

However, do not expect the church to receive you into membership without your repentance from homosexuality, faith in Christ as Lord, and continued practice that gives evidence of that repentance and faith:

• You should move out from living with a homosexual partner and completely break off that and all other such relationships immediately. If your concern is about feelings of love or loneliness, bear in mind that God's love for you is demonstrated by the giving of his only Son to die for you. Once you have placed faith in his Son, God promises that he "will never leave you nor forsake you" (Heb. 13:5). The Lord is able to give you new, God-fearing, loving friends who will walk with you as you seek to live for him. This should be done after sharing with your unsaved, homosexual friends about the love of Christ, so that they can choose as well to accept or reject him. This demonstration of love may be crucial to whether they eventually choose Christ themselves or not.

• You must avoid homosexual bars, clubs, and similar gathering places common to the homosexual community. This includes gatherings of metrosexuals, bisexuals, transgender individuals, so-called homosexual churches, and homosexual-welcoming churches. This may seem extreme. However, if you were an alcoholic desiring to repent from alcohol abuse, repentance would include staying away from bars, liquor stores, liquor aisles in grocery and convenience stores, keg and drinking parties, and even a glass of alcoholic beverage with a meal. You would stay away from drinking buddies and fellow alcoholics who might offer you a drink until you were free enough from the desire for alcohol to resist drinking and could lead others to do the same. This staying away is not meant to condemn those places or people. Instead it is meant to provide the proper environment for you to be free from distractions that may take your focus away from God as you attempt to cultivate new habits.

• You must destroy all homosexual, erotic, and pornographic literature, audio and visual media, and paraphernalia in your possession. A great portion of your battle to turn away from sin will be mental: your mind must be able to tell your feelings and desires the truth about God, his righteous standards, his power, and his love for you. As a Christian, one is called to live a new life and to develop a new way of thinking based on the death and resurrection of Christ and the power to live a new life that comes from believing on Christ:

> I appeal to you therefore, brothers, by the mercies of God, to present your bodies as a living sacrifice, holy and acceptable to God, which is your spiritual worship. Do not be conformed to this world, but be transformed by the renewal of your mind, that by testing you may discern what is the will of God, what is good and acceptable and perfect. (Rom. 12:1–2)

> Now this I say and testify in the Lord, that you must no longer walk as the Gentiles do, in the futility of their minds. They are darkened in their understanding, alienated from the life of God because of the ignorance that is in them, due to their hardness of heart. They have become callous and have given themselves up to sensuality, greedy to practice every kind of impurity. But that is not the way you learned Christ!—assuming that

you have heard about him and were taught in him, as the truth is in Jesus, to put off your old self, which belongs to your former manner of life and is corrupt through deceitful desires, and to be renewed in the spirit of your minds, and to put on the new self, created after the likeness of God in true righteousness and holiness. (Eph. 4:17–24)

• If in your life as a homosexual you chose to develop gender-marking characteristics typical of a person of the opposite sex, such as a change in tone of voice, a cadence or flare to your walk, a drastic alteration of your hair, or adorning yourself with clothing and jewelry common to the other gender, you must choose to stop using these markers. You must not send signals to homosexuals that you are continuing to deny your natural gender. While God "looks at the heart" more than one's outward appearance (1 Sam. 16:7), he is concerned about men and women having appearances appropriate for each gender (see Deut. 22:5; 1 Cor. 11:14–15; 1 Tim. 2:9–10; 1 Pet. 3:3–6).

• You need to publicly declare your repentance among the people of God and to seek out those who can help you walk in maturity. Christians are to "bear one another's burdens" (Gal. 6:2). You will need people to help you carry the load of the struggle of attempting to be free from homosexual desires. You will also need people to encourage you to continue to fight to overcome sin, to pray for you, and to be available if you fall back into your old habits while attempting to gain victory over homosexuality. Such people will be there to support you, reminding you that God forever forgives those who humbly confess and start over rightly with him.

You should not be upset because the church has standards for membership. You cannot force your standards, or the standards of popular culture, on the church. The church should not and must not accept unrepentant homosexuals—or unrepentant sinners of any type of transgressions—into membership.

The church did not make the rules for her standards of conduct. The one true God, who is holy in all of his ways, made the standards. It is he who calls you to believe on Jesus Christ so that he can give you salvation from your sins. He offers you Christ so that you can become a sinner saved by grace who lives holy among God's people, the church.

So if it is acceptance you are seeking, go to Jesus first. Once you have met him in repentance, all of the other redeemed sinners will be glad to accept you!

FOR FURTHER STUDY

Ash, Christopher. *Marriage: Sex in the Service of God.* Leicester, UK: Inter-Varsity, 2003.

Heimbach, Daniel R. *True Sexual Morality: Recovering Biblical Standards for a Culture in Crisis.* Wheaton, IL: Crossway Books, 2004.

Schmidt, Thomas E. *Straight and Narrow: Compassion and Clarity in the Homosexual Debate.* Downers Grove, IL: InterVarsity Press, 1995.

NOTE

[1] It is recognized that the trustworthiness of this account as Scripture is textually disputed. For more, see D. A. Carson, *The Gospel According to John: An Introduction and Commentary* (Grand Rapids, MI: Eerdmans, 1991), 333–337.

ABOUT THE AUTHOR

Rev. Eric C. Redmond is Pastor of Hillcrest Baptist Church in Temple Hills, Maryland, where he began serving in 2001. Prior to the pastorate, Rev. Redmond was Assistant Professor of Bible and Theology at Washington Bible College, Lanham, Maryland. He serves on the Trustee Board of Southwestern Baptist Theological Seminary, Ft. Worth, Texas and the Executive Board of the National African American Fellowship of the Southern Baptist Convention, and he maintains membership in the Evangelical Theological Society. He holds degrees from Washington Bible College and Dallas Theological Seminary. In 2007–2008 he served as the Second Vice President of the Southern Baptist Convention.

Rev. Redmond and his wife, Pamela, reside in Lanham, Maryland, with their five children—Charis, Chloe, Candace, Calvin, and Codell. Together, Pastor and Mrs. Redmond have provided ministry to college students and young married couples. The heart of the Redmonds' ministry partnership is strengthening marriages.

PERSONAL NOTES

PERSONAL NOTES

PERSONAL NOTES

PERSONAL NOTES

PERSONAL NOTES

PERSONAL NOTES

PERSONAL NOTES